take
time
to be
_____brief

Paberback ISBN: 979-8-9867211-2-5
ePub ISBN: 979-8-9867211-3-2

Library of Congress Control Number (LCCN): 2023903043

Good Soil Press
St. Paul, Minnesota

Cover and interior design:
The Brand Office

AJ HOFSTETTER

take
time
to be
_____brief

exploring the art of being heard

Good Soil Press

acknowledgements

To Rachel ___ it's insane that you still believe in me. Just insane. Without you, I'd have given up any notion of belief long ago.

To my team ___ the crew at The Brand Office, who make me look better than I am as we work as brand strategists together. Especially to Kendal, who stepped out on the agency adventure with me, and to Steve, who showed me that even guys like us can write books.

To my readers ___ of all the choices in things to read and things to do with your time, you've chosen these pages. For that, I'm grateful. And I hope it produces life in everything you touch.

TABLE OF CONTENTS

take time to be brief.

THIS STATEMENT comes loosely from a quote you've probably heard before, often attributed to people like Blaise Pascal, Mark Twain, or Winston Churchill, among others. The quote is this, or something like it:

If I had more time, I would have written
a shorter letter.

And, incidentally, my statement (and subsequently the title to this work) came to me in an effort to say that could-have-been-Twain quote with more brevity.

Take Time to Be Brief.

The phrase is actually my tagline in the work that I do as a brand strategist and creative director for a Twin Cities brand and marketing agency. It's the standard I have when helping companies and clients figure out how to talk about themselves. It's the journey they go on to discover who they are, so that ultimately, they can build systems and standards for communication for their brand.

Most often, I describe that process in this way: "Say it as many times as you need to say it so you can say it right the first time."

Go ahead and read that again if you need to.

The idea is self-explanatory if you take a moment to unpack it. Being concise only happens when you're being intentional, and being intentional is hard work that will probably take some time. Putting in the work is a commitment that's going to cost you in time, energy, and resources. It may mean that you have to let go of ideas you've always held close. It may change your timing for a project or launch, and it often brings conflicts (both internal and external) to the surface. Being brief, whether in marketing, speaking, or socializing, means you've thought about what you're saying.

It's easier—and even faster—to be wordy.

I have a pretty decent sense that when this book is finished, published, and distributed, I'll read it and cringe at all the words I used that I didn't need to use. Like, for instance, the last word or two of that last sentence. And I've worked hard to keep my word count down because a 600-page manifesto on brevity could be a hit to my credibility.

The reality of content development and communication philosophy, however, is that you are never going to arrive. I've discovered—and maybe decided—that destinations are exceedingly rare, both in communication and in life. Whether in business or at home, in relationships or in bank accounts, reaching a certain goal rarely frees us to stop, to call it "good." It's not going to be enough to get the job, make the money, cross the threshold, or own the land. A new, loftier goal supplants the first. Once you get to where you're going, the goalpost moves further out.

And so it is with good messages: not a destination, but still a goal.

The pursuit of brevity is a perpetual process where you never really arrive at completeness. That's because brevity isn't science. It's art. As soon as you get to a good place, something changes. Whether it's because the word you thought was perfect is actually missing the mark or because your message needs to adapt to your changing product or mission, you inevitably have to step back to find the right way to say what needs to be said. Taking time to be brief means you're continually sharpening, clarifying, and shaping your message. It means you're perpetually viewing communication as something that's *intentional*.

How We'll Get There

The word brevity, as it relates to language, is defined as "the quality of expressing much in few words" (dictionary.com).

The only way to know if what you're saying is essential is by putting in some hard work. Some of which (but not all) we'll outline in the pages that follow. The words on these pages are my effort to facilitate some of the steps you need to take in your effort to be effective in your communication. It's a sort of manifesto on communication—my effort to put into words (hopefully not too many of them) exactly what I do so that more people start thinking this way in the work they do, the speeches they give, the sermons they preach, the questions they ask, the conversations they have, and the lives they live.

A Few Thoughts and Disclaimers:

1. I'm not an expert at brevity, especially if you get me talking. I often say, with all the false humility I can muster, "I can talk all day. It's just a matter of saying something." Lazy talkers are long talkers, and precise talkers don't get there by accident. For me and the work I do, brevity is both a goal and a moving target. It's something that I talk about not because I'm *good* at it, but because I value it and am learning to make it a part of my life.

2. Brevity isn't about using fewer words; it's about using *better* words. And usually, when you use better words, you end up using fewer. If we can say it simpler—which we probably can—then we should. So don't think of brevity as saying less. Think of it as saying more with less. Or maybe simply *saying better*.

3. Brevity is more about the perspective you have than it is about a sentence you write. Brevity is, always has been, and always will be, evolutionary. What's brief today may be wordy tomorrow. For me, creating the habit of brevity doesn't mean that I always say it right the first time. In fact, I never do. Instead, it's created in me a sort of system for thinking and communicating. I find new and better ways to say things because I'm actually thinking about what I'm saying, what I mean by the words I'm choosing, what others could *think* I mean by them, and how I could speak more effectively. Brevity is just as much a methodology for effective communication as it is a frame of mind and a way of life.

4. Brevity is not silence; it's intentionality. A pursuit of brevity is not an excuse to stay quiet. Only fools should keep silent. And with that, brevity doesn't mean that there aren't times to go long. It simply points to intentionality—choosing to communicate *what's essential.* Sometimes it takes a long time to say what's essential. But imagine how long an essential message becomes if you don't take time to be brief!

We'll eventually get there by discovering and determining what's essential in our message and then creating the standards for representing those pieces to the audience. The goal here is not perfection. It's to get us all to stop and think and then think again (and then again) before being so eager to speak. If we can stop and think before we dive in to saying our piece, we'll discover countless opportunities to be sharper, cleaner, clearer, and quicker.

introduction___

I REMEMBER sitting in an auditorium full of business people at a leadership conference. It was one of
those all-day workshop-type events covering a wide
range of business topics, starting in a corporate session with a keynote speaker. After his introduction,
the keynote approached the podium and, as part of
his opening, made the following request: "I'd love
it if I could just ask everybody to put their phones
down for these next 25 minutes." He wanted people's
undivided attention and, to his credit, wanted us to
get the most out of our time at the event. This was
an opportunity to learn, to be inspired, and to grow.
And he knew that phones compete for loyalty and
attention while also fatiguing our minds.

I wish I remembered the presentation that followed, but I don't. I'm not trying to be hard on the guy. I know where he was coming from. But it turns out that his request is the only thing I remember about him and his presentation. I knew I didn't agree with his initial premise: that putting down a phone would remove distraction. My brain was all the evidence I needed to refute that. But secondly, and more importantly, something felt off about the responsibility he was putting on my shoulders. Should it really be *my* responsibility, as the listener, to put down distractions and be engaged with his talk?

It seems to me that a more ideal scenario would be that he would have taken it upon himself to captivate my attention, to make my phone the less attractive option. Make me laugh. Make me cry. Make me think. Make me dream. Was he expecting too much of his listeners? Wouldn't a strong and captivating communicator draw me in regardless of my texts, emails, and task lists?

Without getting into the unnecessary back and forth, his request left me with questions about communication that I'm still trying to answer. As a writer and communicator by trade, I wonder if it's fair for me to have these kinds of expectations in my own communication. Does a good communicator expect people to remove distractions, or does a good communicator make people forget they even have a phone? Maybe it's both. Or maybe it's somewhere in the middle.

Ultimately, it brings out a more fundamental question: How would I describe a *good* communicator?

Some will say it's about delivery and presentation, whether something is convincing, entertaining, or memorable. Some might say it's about style—asserting that a Morgan Freeman or James Earl Jones-type speaker is better than a soft-spoken communicator with a forgettable voice. Others say it's a matter of preparation or mastery of content.

Obama for America

For those paying attention in 2012, you'll remember the energy and life surrounding the *Obama for America* campaign.

Whatever your political leaning, you'll likely acknowledge that Barack Obama's first presidential bid was marked with a previously unexperienced measure of energy and life. Obama for America 2012 raised more money, activated more donors, engaged more voters, and recruited more volunteers than any other candidate. The data they captured leading up to and during the campaign became the source of all of their decision-making, down to which subject lines they'd use for their emails (subject lines that spanned from "Put Michelle in the White House" to "hey…"). Their process for soliciting financial contributions involved methods and strategies that hadn't been tried before. And at the very heart of it all—within their precision and sophistication—was a gifted orator, a charismatic centerpiece. Barack Obama worked crowds over almost as if he was shooting from the hip with his messages of hope and change. It even landed him a Nobel Prize.

But be confident of this: There was absolutely no "shooting from the hip" in that campaign, at least not where it mattered. His inspiring words and hope-infused optimism were not random nor were they the natural overflow of a charismatic leader and eternal optimist. What looked effortless and energetic on the outside was deeply methodical and detailed within. It was the most impressive use of data and strategy we'd seen in the political space, and it produced the most effective results.

The Obama 2012 campaign would ultimately become the most successful political effort of any that had come before it, both in terms of reach and contributions.

If you feel like taking the time, do the research. It's fascinating and dripping with insights (Find the "Inside the Cave: Obama's Digital Campaign" slide deck online).

So Who Deserves the Credit for the Success of Obama's Campaign?

A great question. Many would contend that Obama himself deserves most of the credit. He was likable, approachable, and seemingly authentic. He was a candidate that people felt they could connect with. He smoked cigarettes, drank pilsener, and shot hoops in his driveway. I do some of those things. He laughed at funny jokes and rolled his eyes at lame ones. He lamented the challenges of father- hood and even made fun of himself. He kept his cool and didn't take the bait of his mudslinging counterparts.

But by itself, that's not enough. What about his message? What about his audience? What about his rousing speeches and those packed-out events? What about the hundreds of millions of dollars (nearly twice the amount of Romney) that his campaign raised?

Maybe his strategists deserve the credit. Strategy is powerful when you do something with it. Without action, however, strategy is just a really expensive, albeit optimistic, conversation. It needs motion to matter. At the end of the day, a great strategy that's poorly implemented will be beaten out every time by a mediocre one that's well-executed.

So maybe it was the social media team or speech writers. But then, they're at the mercy of the message that's being built and broadcast. And those messages are at the mercy of the source and data behind the message, the researchers and analytics that constructed and tested various concepts, and the communication platforms that distributed them. So then maybe it was the web team who built out the contribution platforms and high-performing websites. Of course it's not that.

Forgive me. I've not been brief.

And you get the point.

It wasn't a single decision or division of the campaign. It wasn't a candidate, a software, or a tagline. It was deeper—more integral and foundational than any one component or any one cog in the machine.

It came down to hard work.

And Hard Work Is the Foundation for Any Communication That Ultimately Does the Job.

It can be difficult to nail down a single, universally agreeable, concise definition of a good communicator because you have to know what you're measuring. Are you basing it off of how many people are reached, what kind of response is evoked, how much of the message is articulated, or some other quantifiable result? A logical metric to consider as a defining quality of good communication is *effectiveness*.

A good communicator effectively delivers an intended message to its intended audience.

Every word of that sentence is important.

Good communication is best defined as effective communication *because it does its job*. It accomplishes its purpose. It says the thing it's supposed to say and does the thing it's supposed to do. It's more than being sleeker or louder than competing messages, and it's bigger than the platform from which it's communicated. It's the fruit of hard work. It requires commitment, along with scrappiness and a decent amount of data. And then it requires that you know what to do with all that you discover.

Saying Much More with Much Less

In the pages that follow, we'll unpack the posture and process for effective communication as it can be understood for individuals and organizations. It's not a comprehensive breakdown of every facet or detail. It's not a tutorial on speechwriting or speech giving. Good communication comes down to more than creativity, charisma, or punchiness.

What you do with the words in these pages is going to depend on who you are, what kind of platform and message you're building, and why communication matters to you. Ideally, it makes you a better communicator anywhere you go, from your kitchen table to board rooms and billboards. Ideally, it makes you more intentional and thoughtful, giving you a renewed appreciation for listening and for the people on the other side of your words.

Hopefully, the words that follow will give you *the ability to say much more with much less.*

The process is best accomplished with 4 distinct, iterative, and interdependent components of your message:

___knowing you (chapter 1)

There's a process of discovery and research that makes knowing what needs to be said easier. There's no secret sauce, silver bullet question, or magical key to unlock it. The process isn't rocket science, and a million different brand professionals have a million different pathways to get you there. Some are better than others. But whatever method you employ, the goal is the same:

Know your message because once you know it, you can start building your framework for communicating.

___ knowing your audience (chapter 2)

Knowing your audience is the beginning of communicating what you've just discovered. The seemingly most insignificant of influences can drastically alter a message. Your audience will make assumptions and connections based on the lives they've lived, the experiences they've had, the educations they've received, the biases they grew up with, the baggage they've picked up...and the list goes on. You have to know them if you're going to talk to them. And if you don't know them, you'll miss them.

___ choosing your words (chapter 3)

Why say in 10 words what you can say in 9, unless the 10th word is essential? And why say in 1000 words what didn't need to be said at all? Making the right choices for your message makes effectiveness possible because it means that the words you use are being used *on purpose.* This process of choosing your words means you're looking at your own communication style and your audience's listening style. It means that you learn to be more intentional in speaking so you can be heard.

___being brief (chapter 4)

This is where you exercise your ability to do more with less. All the work put into understanding who you are and who you're talking to shows its value when you can communicate effectively. It means that you're able to say it well. It means that you're comfortable with silence and willing to ask questions. And it means that you're discovering that brevity isn't about what you *aren't* saying but about what you *are* saying.

Putting in the Work

The summary of everything we're about to cover essentially comes down to the idea that good messages take time. Effective communicators have to be willing to put in hard work.

Each chapter of this book will end with a "Putting in the Work" section. These sections are not a step-by-step guide to brand discovery and communication, and just like everything else in this space, there are multiple pathways to the same place. These sections are simply intended to open your mind to thinking differently about the message you're trying to capture and convey. They're intended to get you thinking and moving. They're intended to facilitate a conversation about how to be less lazy, more intentional, and more effective in your communication.

Just like we saw in 2012, effective communication doesn't happen on the fly or from the hip, and it's not a guarantee, no matter how soothing the voice or inspirational the message. It happens in a million moments leading up to that moment, in the effort you've put into finding, building, and communicating your message. It's found in the work you've put into discovering your message and in the commitment you've made to sticking to it.

Being heard is an art form. When communication is done right, it makes speaking easier for you and listening easier for your audience.

an apple a day
knowing you____

Telling a story is like reaching into a granary
full of wheat and drawing out a handful.
There is always more to tell than can be told.

—WENDELL BERRY, *Jayber Crow*

I WAS PULLING INTO the parking lot of a strip mall in my small Oregon town when I saw a sign in the window of our local bookstore. It was well lit, positioned as the focal point, but yet so subtle that I assume many missed it: "*Don't judge a book by its movie.*"

Brilliant. Absolutely brilliant. I love punchy statements. I love messages that take readers on a journey. The only thing I hated about that sign and its message was that I didn't think of it.

I still love that message, almost 20 years after first seeing it, for reasons far beyond its surprise ending. I love that it recognizes the intrinsic challenges that come with identifying and communicating essential pieces of a story.

Telling a Story

The chasm between a book and its movie has been the source of much angst.

When it comes to storytelling, I could give you a pretty good rundown of Tolkien's *Lord of the Rings* series. I could tell you the general plot of Clancy's political thrillers and about a hundred other books. But that's not because I've read them. It's because I've watched the movies. And if you ask anyone who's read the books, they'll tell you that I'm missing out.

I believe them.

The truth is that I've never been a very strong reader of fiction. Maybe it's my easily distracted brain or some lack of creativity or capacity, but my mind can't seem to keep up. I drift off, lose track, and fight to stay in it. I mix up characters and their backstories. I trail off into my own imaginings. It's not from a lack of effort or good advice or suggestions from others. I've picked up Tolkien and Dostoevsky a dozen or so times. I've also tried going lighter or more mainstream. I've tried pacing myself. I've tried reading in the morning and at night. I've committed to all sorts of books and authors. I've finished some, but only a fraction of those I've started. I've never accomplished much—at least when it comes to fiction.

And so the idea that a movie almost never captures the richness of its written predecessor makes me realize that I'm missing out on a lot of quality storytelling. Look again at Wendell Berry's words that started this section:

"Telling a story is like reaching into a granary full of wheat and drawing out a handful. There is always more to tell than can be told."

The truth is simple: You can't possibly include it all. It's up to you, as the storyteller and messenger, to decide what to keep in, what to leave out, and how to deliver it to the people listening. If you're going to do that well, you have to do the hard work of discovery. You have to know the story forward and backward. You have to know it intimately—every detail and every pivotal moment. You have to know the essential pieces of each essential piece. And then you have to work through it again and again until what's essential is what's articulated, and until what's articulated is what's understood.

You have to put in the work.

Why You're Not Brief

If you're like me, you struggle with brevity not because of something you're doing but because of a whole series of things you're *not* doing. You're not putting in the hard work of understanding your message. You're not sold on the "essential" piece of your message, and so you're trying to make everything essential. You're not content to say it quickly because you're still living and speaking in the belief that the more you talk, the more you're saying. You're not comfortable in silence or confident in your audience and their ability to draw the right conclusions.

If you're being honest, you can probably identify multiple areas of your life where you struggle with brevity. Poor communication isn't reserved for extroverts. Whether you're working a room or sitting silent in the corner, clarity is nothing more than the natural outcome of knowing who you are.

Maybe you're like me and often find yourself with post-social-interaction regret. You wish you'd have asked more questions and not dominated so many conversations. You wish you'd let other people talk or spent time learning from others. You grieve the way you stumbled through the answer to that question or you kick yourself for losing your train of thought and getting off script.

Fortunately, as I work through my own posture of brevity, these regrets are becoming less frequent. But being wordy or unclear isn't about what you have *too much of* in your mind or on your tongue; rather, it's what you have *too little* of. Using more words than you need to—whether in socializing, public speaking, or marketing—is usually an indication of a lack of something.

An Understanding of Who You Are

When we lack an understanding of who we are and how we're unique, we struggle to be brief. We might make ourselves into what others expect of us, or we may morph our identity and mission to align with who we think we should be based on others' feedback. With uncertainty in identity comes ambiguity in communication.

Confidence in Your Message

Sometimes we know who we are and what we want to communicate but still question the authority, relevance, or impact of our message. If we're not sure that the things we want to say will be well received or easily believed, we might oversell it. We'll give too many illustrations and go down too many rabbit trails, all in an effort to prove our point.

Trust in Your Audience

This is where the majority of overselling happens. We don't trust our audience to draw the right conclusions. We don't believe they understand our point or make the connections we've intended. We'll tend to think our audience needs us much more than they do, and subsequently, we say too much in our effort to meet those needs.

Usually, our lack of brevity isn't because of one of these, but instead, because of *all* of these, each emerging in varying degrees at different times. Your lack of knowledge, restraint, and trust are making you say more than you need to say and communicate things you don't want to communicate.

An Apple a Day

Stories are told that when Benjamin Franklin read something, he'd seek to know it so well that he could eventually summarize what he'd read in just a few words. No matter how complex and no matter how specialized the discipline, he worked hard to make sure he could capture the essence of something in as few words as possible. Take a look through his publication *Poor Richard's Almanack* and see the many historical and philosophical statements that he penned. His discipline for summarizing became possible not because of his knack for word-smithing but because of his willingness to dive deep, think, understand, and then speak.

When it comes to being effective, simplicity is essential. And simplicity is the product of hard work.

Consider the following statement:

> To live a long and healthy life, a well-balanced diet and regular, sustained activity is essential, statistically increasing both the quantity of a person's days as well as the quality of them, as a regular intake of healthy food along with consistent choices for good sleep, managed anxiety, and physical activity build and reinforce the immune system, engage muscles, restore cognitive health and physiological capacity, decrease atrophy, improve dexterity and nerve and muscle responsiveness, and improve overall performance of both the immunological and physiological functions of the human body over the course of a lifetime.

Phew. Now catch your breath and consider the next statement:

> An apple a day keeps the doctor away.

Both informative. Both saying the same thing. But not both repeatable, consumable, or memorable. While not everything you say or write needs to be punchy (much less rhyme), it does all need to be thought out.

The point is a simple one: Once you really know what needs to be said, you have the opportunity—and the responsibility—to say it better.

So there's the first step: Know what needs to be said.

Without that long statement about healthy choices (or something like it), the common English proverb of "an apple a day" couldn't and wouldn't exist. With the lengthy version comes, intrinsically connected to it, the opportunity to say it better.

PUTTING IN THE WORK

The *effectiveness* of your message is a reflection of how clearly you understand the *essentials* of your message. You have to be able to articulate who you are—even if it takes you an hour to do it.

Define Your Message
Have you taken time to truly define your message? If it's a book you want to write, a speech you want to give, a product you want to launch, or a company you want to start, how well can you articulate who you are and how you're unique in a crowded marketplace?

Differentiate Your Voice
A good way to know if you're confident in articulating your message or brand is by asking yourself a simple question: "Why would someone choose to listen to me?" This question goes immediately to the distinction of your message and brand amongst the many competing voices. If you can't answer that question well, you're going to lack confidence in the strength of your message to stand on its own.

From a place of definition and differentiation, you can begin to find confidence in your voice. It's when you can articulate who you are and how you're different from the other voices you're competing against that you can begin the process of communicating with clarity and effectiveness.

there's beer in the fridge

knowing your audience ___

READ THE TITLE to this section again. What is it saying? If you were in my home and I said that to you, what would I *actually* be telling you?

There's beer in the fridge.

Am I telling you to help yourself? To get me a beer or to not worry about yours because there's already some here? Am I answering a question? Asking one? Am I making a joke? Giving a warning? A dozen or so messages can be pulled from that 5-word statement. The meaning of the statement depends on who I am, who you are, and the context of our situation and relationship.

That's the thing about communication. You have to know more than what *you're* trying to say. You have to also know who's listening and what they'll think you mean. You have to know the *before and after* of the message, how what you say will be received, what messages could be misconstrued, and what assumptions could be made. Don't say the wrong thing by making the wrong choice. You have to be able to anticipate what your audience might misunderstand—even if it's just one wrong word.

Effective communication is not measured in your ability to say what needs to be said but in your ability to know what needs to be heard...and then in crafting your message accordingly.

In leadership, race relations, family dynamics, workplace interactions, with your mechanic or a crabby customer service rep...the list goes on: There's never a time that the recipient of the message shouldn't be considered.

Essential Context

You'd know a lot more about what I mean by, "There's beer in the fridge" if you know more about the context of the statement. Where am I when I say it? What's my story? Who am I saying it to? What's their story?

Context helps you know what you should say and what you shouldn't. It gives parameters to your words and even your body language and tone.

In Relationships

My wife, Rachel, and I have gone to marriage counseling regularly for half a decade. There was a time and a season when therapy was pulling us out of a dismal place. There are still times when therapy is a chance for us to catch our breath and regain perspective. There have been lighthearted sessions and heavy ones. Through it all, we've made it a regular part of our lives because it keeps us on the same page. This every-other-week commitment gives us a chance to do the hard work of making marriage all that it can be. And truthfully, sometimes counseling is just an excuse to get away from our kids and remember that it used be just us—and that it will be again (assuming our kids move out some day).

After one particular counseling session, my wife and I stopped at the grocery store on our way home and began to reflect on all we'd just talked through. I wish I could remember the exact topic because context would be helpful. But at one point in the discussion, I said something like this to Rachel: "When you do that, it makes me feel like you're giving up on our marriage."

Her response was chilling. "How can you give up on a marriage that isn't going anywhere?"

I was devastated. I had seen such progress. We'd healed from so much—or at least had begun to heal. We'd come so far. We were learning to communicate on topics that used to be off limits. We were doing the hard work of making marriage more than something we simply survive. We even dared to expect it to be something we enjoy. And now, hearing her say that it wasn't going anywhere left me without bearings. I was shocked, hurt, and disoriented.

Rachel saw devastation on my face—because I usually wear every emotion except happiness on my sleeve—and asked me a question that I perceived to be equally chilling. "Why does that bother you?"

What could she possibly mean? Why does it bother me? How could it *not* bother me? Why does it *not* bother her? All this work we're doing and now she flippantly remarks that we're on a dead-end street. If our marriage isn't going anywhere, why go to counseling? Why the charade? Why even try?

I'll never forget what she said next. "A.J., I don't understand how that bothered you. I just told you that our marriage isn't going anywhere, that it's here to stay, and that nobody and nothing can change that, and you're discouraged?"

Turns out, there was more than one way to hear what she said. I'm not sure I've ever experienced such polarized interpretations of a single statement. The same words, intonations, *and even context on some level* produced two totally different conclusions. One said, "We're going nowhere" and the other, "We're going everywhere, and we're going there together."

My mind, which is already more prone to a glass-half-empty perspective than hers, interpreted my wife's words in a way that she absolutely never meant them.

On Issues of Race

As the trauma and ensuing chaos of the George Floyd murder took center stage and as the tensions surrounding racism became more palpable (particularly for me in my white, suburban life outside of Minneapolis), I remember having a lot of conversations about race. Almost all of these conversations were with friends and colleagues who have similar amounts of money in their bank accounts and melanin in their skin. The conversations varied from highly emotional to historically thorough. Some admittedly sounded terribly bigoted if someone were listening in. Others sounded hopeless or at the very least confused. But a common point of discussion was around the statement "black lives matter." *For the record, I am speaking here specifically of the statement and am not making any reference to the organization that goes by that name, as I've not researched it and am making no judgments or assertions about it. Further, I use the distinctions here of "black" and "white" for the purpose of engaging in the dialogue as its been laid out through the events of the past few years in our country, since the whiteness of my skin is probably better described as tan (which is a shade of brown) and the blackness of others' skin is better described as, well, also a shade of brown.*

Within those conversations that I had and those like them, there was an unfortunate alternative to the statement "black lives matter" that began to circulate. It said, "All lives matter." I truly believe that most of the people proposing this variation were well-intentioned. It's a true statement after all. All lives do, in fact, matter. And while many of my friends and family members have some level of compassion toward people of a different race, even if they can't necessarily understand or empathize with their plight, that statement is painfully and poorly worded.

I'd contend that it moves us backward as a people.

The problem with the "all lives matter" alternative to the "black lives matter" statement is that it never has seemed to me that the majority of the black community is saying that white people *don't* matter. We don't need to say all lives matter because we already know that white lives do. What the statement "black lives matter" is saying is probably closer to "black lives matter *too*." It's not putting people of color higher than anyone. It's bringing them equal. I remember hearing comedian Michael Jr. propose this alternative to the statement early on in this discussion and only wish more people like me would adapt their thinking to include this essential three-letter modifier.

As a white man, if I choose to clarify that ALL lives matter, I'm not actually hearing or understanding the issue. I'm not concerning myself with the cry of the person on the other side of the conversation. I'm responding out of my own narrative—and probably even my own fear. I'm defending something, and I'm probably assuming a whole lot.

Similarly, I remember vividly a conversation I had with my friend Marius Massie. Marius, an African-American man who spends his life committed to helping individuals, organizations, and companies identify and work through conflict, has done a lot of work in the area of race relations here in the Twin Cities as well as across the country. As he and

I spoke about these topics during the height of our city's and country's turmoil, I remember the topic of white privilege coming up. I told him that the word "privilege" provoked me to defensiveness, implying that I don't deserve my house or my job, inferring that I haven't worked hard to be where I am or that I should feel guilty for things that other's decide I don't *deserve*. More simply, the statement makes me feel unjustly targeted, judged, and treated.

Marius, leading with empathy and a clear understanding of the complexities of human relationship, proposed his own alternative to that term. He changed the conversation. He asked me, "How would you feel if I talked to you about 'white advantage'?"

At that point, everything in my paradigm changed.

Could I acknowledge that there were certain *advantages* to being white? Absolutely. I could think of a few immediately. I never worry about where my wallet is when I am pulled over by the police. And speaking of that, I'm only pulled over by the police when I deserve to be pulled over by the police. I believe I could come up with a pretty decent list of advantages to my life because of the color of my skin within a few minutes. These aren't advantages I chose and not even advantages that I've intentionally exploited or lorded over others. They are, however, intrinsically connected to me. Some of them would seem insignificant. Others would have profound implications.

In that moment, for the first time ever, I believe I was actually having a conversation about white privilege as it's meant to be understood.

By changing the way he framed the idea of white privilege, Marius broke down my walls. He built a bridge over chaos (his term, not mine) and helped me understand what he (and I assume the African American community) really mean when they say that I've been on the receiving end of white privilege.

Context makes all the difference in communication. Communication isn't about saying what needs to be said. It's about knowing what needs to be heard. Our unwillingness to see how our words may misrepresent what we mean can easily—and often—create chaos.

Empathy, Context, and Communication

This is where we talk about empathy. Context is not the same as empathy. While empathy is a deeply emotive term, context is a strategic one. A lack of empathy doesn't necessarily make you a bad communicator just like an abundance of empathy doesn't get your point across. But in all of that, the most effective leaders understand that context and empathy go hand-in-hand.

Where many leaders and communicators fall short in this arena is in the dismissal of empathy with blanket statements like, "I can't take time to babysit their emotions" or "I just need them to understand what I mean." Statements like these are indicators that a person is choosing shortcuts and laziness in their language and expecting their audience to do the hard work for them.

The reality is that our job as communicators is, in fact, to babysit the emotions of our audience. It falls within the job description. The hard work belongs to us, the communicators, and the wrong word—and even the wrong tone—is a road block to effective communication. It's not babysitting. It's empathy.

Summary

As we've been saying since the front cover: It takes time to be a good communicator. The more a person considers the story and background of an audience, the more likely he or she is to effectively deliver a message. Whether you're talking about the intricacies and complications of race and marriage or the strategy and sales implications of the right tagline for your business or copy on your website, it's up to you to say not only the words that *you* mean but also the words that *they'll* hear.

After all, much of communication is not really about *what we mean* but about *what they hear.* That's why we have to be intentional about the words we choose. The sooner you identify your audience and understand how their context has impacted their language (and the assumptions and conclusions that go with it), the sooner you can communicate effectively.

Remember, it's not about saying what needs to be said. It's about saying what needs to be heard.

PUTTING IN THE WORK

I remember a job I had a decade or two ago where my boss called me into his office to talk to me about our website. I was put in charge of the project—from both a design and development standpoint as well as a function, purpose, and messaging standpoint. His opinion came at me pretty quickly. He hated our new site. Content was too buried. There was too much white space and the videos were too short. Pictures were too prevalent and there were not enough calls to action. It didn't feel like the websites of other organizations in our industry.

My response to him was a simple one. I asked him the age of our target customer. His answer: between the ages of 16 and 25. I then asked him his age. His answer: north of 70. To his credit, he saw my point. Our website wasn't talking to him, and so I wasn't all that worried about his opinion of it. It was designed to talk to *them*, those 16-25-year-olds who we determined were our audience. If he could have demonstrated that *they* didn't like our site, we'd have a different conversation.

There are three essential steps to this phase of identifying and communicating your message that, if neglected, will be at best ineffective, and at worst, corrosive, to your message.

Identify Your Audience

There's a common exercise you've probably been a part of if you've ever worked on a marketing strategy for a company. Terms like "avatars" and "customer personas" are different ways to define the work of understanding your audience.

When done thoroughly, these customers are given names (albeit, imaginary) and include information like the number of kids they have, the books they read, the places they hang out, and the places they work. This deep dive into creating a figure with whom you can relate is the beginning of understanding the context of your audience.

Learn Their Language

Much of the success you'll experience in communication will come downstream from the work you've put in to studying your audience. When you've learned who they are, you understand their context. You know what matters to them and what stories they resonate with. You also know what words or ideas are roadblocks to them.

Change Your Language

Your willingness to adapt your language to your audience will directly impact your effectiveness. Some of this comes down to strategic decisions made long before you're ever communicating in front of them. Some comes down to real-time decisions. It's measured in your willingness and ability to read the room, be interruptible, and be willing to pivot and adapt your communication style so that your audience is engaged and your message is received.

While it may seem like a lot of work, it's much more work to untangle the messes left from sloppy communication. Knowing who you're talking to *must* change the way you talk, at least if you're interested in being heard.

i would rather be sad then happy

choosing your words _____

I DISPLAYED the title of this chapter as a statement in front of a workshop I taught. It didn't let me down. It caused as much confusion as I'd hoped. Eventually someone read it for what it *actually* said and blurted out something like, "Oh. I see it."

If you haven't discovered what I'm talking about yet, look again.

I'd rather be sad then happy.

In other words, I'd rather be sad first and happy second. Or, to really unpack the statement: if given a choice in my life, I choose to end on a happy note. I'd rather be sad at the beginning, learn the lessons life has for me, make good choices, and then be happy.

If I had written the words, "I'd rather be sad than happy," I'd say you should probably surround yourself with more positive people. Using the wrong word makes you say the wrong thing. The word "than" is a statement of comparison. The word "then" is a statement of order. One says, "I like this more than that." The other says, "I'll have this then I'll have that." Using the word "then" instead of "than" changes absolutely everything about the message and meaning of the statement.

Your Essential Message

The more intentional you are with your words, the more control you have over the outcome of your efforts.

Your brand is one of the things in business and in life that you have the *most* control over. Think of your brand as what other people believe to be true about you. It's like asking someone to describe your house after they've driven past it. What was its curb appeal? What conclusions could they draw about you by what they saw? What do you care about? What did they observe about your values? Your priorities, projects, and pastimes? What are you working on? What are you neglecting?

It's amazing what people can learn about someone simply by observation. It's equally amazing what people can assume.

Control over your messaging and brand is about more than avoiding typos (though that's important), expanding your reach, or having a great tagline, logo, or billboard. It's about knowing what you're trying to say, knowing your audience, and which words, ideas, platforms, and images will most effectively bridge the gaps that exist between those two things.

Reducing the Unnecessary

From a practical standpoint, you could go through a message time and time again and still find unnecessary words. On the other hand, it's easy to overdo it by overthinking it.

The trick is to be intentional in your communication, and in that, to expose the bad habits of filler language and bad habits. Whether it's the constant and frequent use of "like" or "just" or the tendency to end statements with questions like, "Know what I mean?," the chances are high that your language is full of unnecessary words that are stealing from your credibility by burying your message.

Consider the difference between these two statements:

That storm was intense.

That storm was very intense.

The word "very" in the second sentence actually detracts from the statement's message. It puts an unneeded limit on the "intensity" and steals from the strength of the statement. Certainly there are times when such words contribute to a message, such as the use of "somewhat" or "finally." But if we're honest, we use words like these most often not because we're being clear but because we're being unintentional. That's often true of adverbs.

I digress. The purpose here is not to get into a granular discussion of the mechanics of writing, much less my own preferences in language and writing style. The purpose is to challenge you to not clutter your message with words that aren't helping you do the job.

Think about the person you know who goes long in every answer they give. Or consider how often you hear someone use the phrase, "over-exaggerate" when the word "exaggerate" will do. Whether the words you're eliminating are wrong or are simply unnecessary, it's worth doing an inventory of your vocabulary. You'll be amazed (and perhaps a bit ashamed) at the sheer volume of words you use. Or maybe you'll realize that you're cheapening your message by complicating or cluttering it.

None of this means that there's no room for flowery language or elegance in your communication. In fact, when effort is put into eliminating unnecessary words, elegance becomes attainable. And elegance in communication is a gift.

The Possum Rule

> *"Should I abide by the rules until they're changed, or help speed the change by breaking them?"*

—ASHLEIGH BRILLIANT

I was working through some content projects for one of my clients. I had written scripts for a handful of videos they were putting together and some of the marketing pieces that accompanied them. Most of the content was approved without issue. One particular critique, however, got my attention. My client said, "You can't start a sentence with 'Because.'" My response was simple (albeit, a bit condescending): "Because you said that, I won't do it again." To that statement, the response I got back was a simple, "Thanks."

Of course, she had no idea what I'd done in my response. My fully constructed, grammatically on-point statement did, in fact, start with the word "because." But to her point, and in her defense, the sentence she was referencing in her critique was not grammatically correct. It said something like, "Because that's why we're here."

This issue becomes a hangup for many communicators. Whether in speaking or in writing, the rules of grammar are a tricky topic. On one hand, it's good to be consistent and accurate. On the other hand, it's good to be approachable and understandable. To fall 100% on the side of grammar will eventually lead to some tricky—if not outright terrible—communication. There are times grammatically when you should say "whom" instead of "who," but that doesn't mean it's a good idea. There are many who consider it to be bad form or just plain sloppy to start sentences with "there" or use words like "got." And there are others who are critiquing the first word to this exact sentence.

For those who are proficient in writing—knowing the rules of grammar and standards for sentence structure—proper grammar easily gets in the way of strong messaging. They won't approve a tagline because it ends with a preposition or doesn't resolve properly. They won't use a linking verb without a predicate nominative. They keep to the rules and weaken their impact. The rules of language are everywhere, and so when it comes to messaging, you have to balance the rules of grammar with the goals of communication.

This is something I call the Possum Rule.

The Possum Rule gives you permission to break the rules of grammar for the purposes of effective communication. Think about people who insist on calling them *opossums*. Technically they're right, but they're wrong on so many levels. Anyone who spells it "opossum" (or even worse, pronounces it that way) is far too committed to correctness. Only people working careers in zoology should be allowed to pronounce it that way.

The summary is simple: Break the rules of grammar when they interfere with the rules of communication.

On a related note, if anyone knows Joanne Tomasiak, the amazingly talented, profoundly brilliant, circa 1997 English teacher from Chalker High School in Southington, Ohio, who sparked in me a love for writing and language, please don't tell her I said this. She'll never forgive me.

Don't sacrifice effectiveness for the sake of correctness. And don't mistake correctness in one as effectiveness in the other.

Summary

Whether it's dropping words that are unnecessary or choosing words that are effective, the only way to really sharpen your message is to be more committed to good communication than you are to a specific vocabulary.

Choose every word, knowing that the only way to reach your audience is by saying words that mean something *to them*. In doing that, you'll find that effective communication becomes possible.

PUTTING IN THE WORK

A while back, I worked for a tech company. One person I got to know somewhat well from that job was a man named Gus. Gus was always there for great conversations, good lunches, and the ability to know almost every single person in any given room.

One of the things that he did for me was help me identify bad habits in my language. Gus once pointed out to me that I said the words "Know what I mean?" at the end of many of my sentences. He graciously insisted on helping me break this habit despite my pleas that he stop. Whether at lunch, in a car, or during a meeting, you'd hear Gus let out a high-pitched *whoop!* any time I uttered those words. He did this with no regard to our surroundings or the company we were in. It was his way of getting me to realize how much I said the words "Know what I mean?" How generous of him. Truthfully, I still haven't entirely broken the habit of ending sentences with that phrase. I still catch myself doing it, and when I do, I hear a faint *whoop* somewhere in my subconscious.

Consider taking some steps toward stronger communication.

Critique yourself

Find a video or some other recording of yourself (or record a new one). Pay attention to what you notice. Do you sound insecure or nervous? How many "likes" and "ums" do you observe? Unnecessary or filler language? Insensitive or potentially misunderstood words? Did you lose your way?

Find a Gus

Ask someone you trust to help you identify your bad habits and learn new behavior. While they may not belt out an actual *whoop* with every blunder, an external voice helps identify habits that you're close to, and thus, probably blind to. Be advised. This tactic can get annoying (no offense, Gus).

Write It First

If you know what you're wanting to say but recognize that you have a flurry of bad habits and filler words that clutter your message, it helps to write out what you want to say. Once it's written out to your standards, practice saying it the way you wrote it. You'll quickly identify words that don't matter, take you off topic, or aren't quite doing the job.

Good communication doesn't happen on accident. Whether it's a friend to holler "whoop," an invitation for honest feedback from colleagues, or a recording of yourself that you're willing to critique, it's worth finding your bad habits. It's worth removing as many of them as you can so that your audience can hear the message you have for them.

In all of it, the bigger challenge for reaching your audience goes well beyond your own language nuances or inefficiencies. Your most important job here is being willing to use words that matter to your audience. If you're not going to find and use the words that mean the right things to *them*, you're not going to be able to connect them to your essential message.

cowboy coffee
taking time to be brief⸺

ONE OF THE GREATEST uses of storytelling in
advertising is a Toyota commercial called "Cowboy
Coffee." A brief jaunt down the information super-
highway will show you a brilliant, 15-second spot
with almost no voice-over or text on the screen. It's
just a story, told poignantly, that communicates so
much. I revisit it every few months, and I've never
watched it just once.

Every once in a while, I stumble upon this kind of
marketing campaign or brand message. Similar to
that story shared earlier about the bookstore sign
that said, "Don't judge a book by its movie," a message that's well-built and well-delivered inspires
me. It gives me respect (along with a fun-loving

resentment) for the creative minds that have the whit and nerve to put it out there. Whether it's a car commercial, a billboard on the side of the freeway, or an author who says in 15 words what I've struggled my whole life to articulate, I am refreshed by good communication. It's as though a well-articulated message or campaign isn't *created* at all, but rather is simply released from where it was caged.

That's why we take time.

Brevity equals credibility. As the ancient proverb states, "Even fools are thought wise if they keep silent..." (Proverbs 17:8, NLT). How many times have you said the wrong thing because you've used the wrong words? And as a less sacred source tells us, "Better to be thought a fool than to open your mouth and prove it true."

Each step of this process and each section of this book is essential in your pursuit of effective communication. They're interdependent upon one another, as your understanding of who you are is useless without the right words to communicate it. Your knowledge of your audience is useless without the right understanding of who you are and why what you're trying to communicate matters. Each step is a continuing process, and each step is dependent upon the others. A good communicator is always refining their message, malleable to the inevitable changes to come.

Knowing Your Message

How effective are you at summarizing who you are and what you do? If it's a business you're leading, how effective are your employees at summarizing your company and its distinctions? How confident are you that people on every level of your organization could accurately and clearly speak to your mission and purposes?

Or if we're talking about your personal brand or your ability to effectively deliver a speech from a platform...

What about your message is worth listening to? What's essential? What's unnecessary? What are you doing in your communication to add to your credibility? To take from it?

Whether your pursuits are personal or professional, put in the hard work of knowing who you are and what's vital about your message. Say who you are as many times as you need to so that when the time comes, you can say it exactly as you need to.

Knowing Your Audience

Your willingness to consider the context of your audience will determine the impact of your message. If you know who you are, but you don't know who *they* are, you're wasting your breath. And, more unfortunately, their time.

Study them. Know them. Ask them questions. Learn their language. Listen to what they mean and not to what they say.

Choosing Your Words

Be intentional with every message and every word choice. Be aware of clichés, but not afraid of them. In other words, a cliché is only a cliché when we stop believing the words it's made of. If we're using a cliché, it's up to us to either infuse meaning back into the phrase or find a better way to say it. Be aware of sloppy habits. Avoid words that mean something different to your audience than they mean to you. Choose better words instead of more words.

The more intentional you are with the words you use, the more successful you'll be in bridging gaps between you and your audience.

Finding Your Own Version of Brief

This is where the ideas we've been discussing become the most subjective. Brevity for one person doesn't mean brevity for another. It's a constant pursuit that isn't really measured by how quickly you say something but by how effectively you say it. And even after you've chosen to be intentional in your messaging and strategic in your communication, you'll discover that it's still just as easy to go long and be sloppy.

PUTTING IN THE WORK

Brevity is an exercise in restraint and wisdom. It's not a change in vocabulary so much as it is a change in habits. It's an expression of trust in your audience and their ability to draw the right conclusions. It's also an expression of trust in your message and its ability to be relevant and clear.

So, as you consider how the message you care about can be communicated more effectively, there are tools I've used to help me get to what matters most. Just like every other part of this process, this isn't some industry secret or a closely guarded piece of intellectual property. It's just one way. And just as an unexamined life isn't worth living, so also an unexamined message is not worth speaking.

The 3-30-3 Process
The summary of the 3-30-3 process for your message is simple: Build it up so that you can break it down.

The first number represents 3 minutes.
This means that you should try to summarize your core message in 3 minutes. Take what's most important, and put it into a concise 3-minute summary. Whether you write it out, record yourself saying it, or simply recite it in your mind, take everything you've discovered about who you are, what you care about, and your audience, and reduce it to 3 minutes.

The second number is 30 seconds.
This means you should take what you just reduced to 3 minutes and make it no more than 30 seconds. If we were

back on the "apple-a-day" statement, this would be where you take the entire medical journal that you just read and reduce it to that longer summary about the value and benefit of healthy eating and healthy living. It might be wordy or confusing. It might lack a certain finesse. But that doesn't matter. The point is to summarize the big message with a simpler one.

The third number is 3 seconds.
This means you should be able to reduce everything to a simple statement. You should be brief. If you were ask me what I do for a living, I need to be able to tell you in a word or two. From there, I can tell you in a sentence. I can tell you in a paragraph. I can tell you in a conversation. I can tell you in a speech or a series of workshops. I can tell you in a book.

The real value of being able to capture that 3-second version of your message is that you're not starting with everything when talking to someone. You're not inviting someone into your home only to show them that everything you own is in the living room. You're simply giving them the "entry way" version of you. When they're comfortable with that version, you can give them the "come in out of the cold" invitation where they can stay for a few minutes. From there, you can ask them to stay for a while. They could move in eventually, but that's not where you started. You started with something much simpler. And that's because you took time to be brief.

afterword____

IN MY CAREER, I've found more satisfaction and joy in working with a septic company than with an organization or individual promising to change the world. I've had more success with 6 words on a full-page ad than I've had with bottomless budgets and unending timelines. It always comes down to the hard work and to the people who are willing to put in that hard work for their brand and their message.

Your only control when it comes to impact comes down to how aware you are of your message, how informed you are of your audience, and how intentional you are with the words you use to reach them. When those pieces are covered, the impact is officially out of your hands. It moves into the hands of the message itself and to the audience receiving it.

Brevity demonstrates the work you've put in to self-awareness, to intentionality. If you can say it with brevity, it means you've thought about it. In a world where louder voices often attract larger audiences (often to ultimately disappoint), we are in desperate need of people, brands, and organizations who think before they speak. So whether you're speaking personally or professionally, and whether you're talking about what matters to you or what you think should matter to others, don't speak useless words. Don't say in 40 words what could have been said in 12. Don't choose words that you prefer when you could use words your audience prefers. Don't dismiss your own laziness in communication only to critique the laziness of your listeners. Listeners, after all, aren't lazy. They're just not hearing.

What does it mean to be brief?

At the end of this, my hope is that you've come to a simple conclusion: That there's value in the process of being brief, of finding a way to say it better. It's a service to your audience. It's a pathway to elegance in speech and clarity in messaging. It establishes your authority on a topic, and it frees your listeners to receive what they need to receive.

Go back to the definition of good communication that we started with, in our unpacking of Obama's 2008 campaign:

A good communicator effectively delivers an intended message to its intended audience.

Nothing in that definition says anything about being brief. But brevity is missing in that definition not because it doesn't matter. It's because it isn't the goal. Effectiveness is the goal. Good communication is measured by how effective you are at reaching your intended audience with your essential message. Being brief is nothing more than the pathway to make your message less convoluted, less cluttered with unnecessary fillers and lazy habits, and less prone to a watered down version of what's meaningful. It's the path to leaving your audience better than how you found them. It's a path to being heard.

Once you've discovered who you are, learned your audience, and chosen your words, your challenge shifts from *being* brief to *staying* brief. At the beginning of this book, the subtitle reads, "Exploring the Art of Being Heard."

That's what all of this is about. Being heard. Hard work is the only way to make that happen. So take the time. Be brief.

works cited

Berry, Wendell. *Jayber Crow.* Berkeley, CA. Counterpoint, LLC. September 5, 2000.

"Brevity." *Dictionary.com.* Accessed November 11, 2022 from https://www.dictionary.com/browse/brevity.

"Fundraising for the 2012 United States presidential election" Accessed November 11, 2022 from https://www.opensecrets.org/pres12/

"Inside the Cave: Obama's Digital Campaign." *Engage Research.* Accessed November 11, 2022 from https://enga.ge/wp-content/uploads/2018/01/Inside_the_Cave-1.pdf.

Holy Bible—New Living Translation. Tyndale House Publishers, Inc. Copyright 2013. www.newlivingtranslation.com

A J H O F S T E T T E R

is a brand enthusiast and
marketing consultant who
helps individuals and
organizations align who they
are with the messages they
communicate. He and his wife,
Rachel, live in White Bear Lake,
Minnesota with their four
children and two dogs.